Into the Cracks

Other Books Written (or Co-written) by Holly Day

The Book Of
Guitar All-in-One for Dummies
I'm in a Place Where Reason Went Missing (poems)
Insider's Guide to the Twin Cities
Music Theory for Dummies
Music Composition for Dummies
Nordeast Minneapolis: A History
A Perfect Day for Semaphore (poems)
Piano All-in-One for Dummies
The Smell of Snow (poems)
Stillwater, Minnesota: A Brief History
Walking Twin Cities
The Yellow Dot of a Daisy (poems)

Into the Cracks

Poems by

Holly Day

Golden Antelope Press
715 E. McPherson
Kirksville, Missouri 63501
2019

Copyright ©2019 by Holly Day

Cover Image Copyright ©2019 Holly Day

Cover Design by Russell Nelson and Lexie Biggs

All rights reserved. No portion of this publication may be duplicated in any way without the expressed written consent of the publisher, except in the form of brief excerpts or quotations for review purposes.

ISBN: 978-1-936135-69-1 (1-936135-69-8)

Library of Congress Control Number: 2019940151

Published by:
Golden Antelope Press
715 E. McPherson
Kirksville, Missouri 63501

Available at:
Golden Antelope Press
715 E. McPherson
Kirksville, Missouri, 63501
Phone: (660) 665-0273
http://www.goldenantelope.com
Email: ndelmoni@gmail.com

To Nancy

Acknowledgements:

- "The Arrogant Imposter" appeared in *Amulet*, vol. 10, no. 92
- "Bleeding the Brakes Dry" appeared in *Amulet*, vol. 10, no. 93
- "Crossing Guard" appeared in *Iota Magazine*, issue 82
- "Dacnomania" appeared in *Et Cetera*, vol. 70, no. 4
- "The Dreams of Tiny Things" appeared in *Beyond Centauri*, vol. 8, no. 4
- "Functional" appeared in *Common Ground Review*, vol. 14, no.1
- "Good Old Me" appeared in *The Alembic*, vol. 94
- "Happily" appeared in *Real: Regarding Arts and Letters*, vol. 36, no.1
- "The Hatchlings" appeared in *Cold Mountain Review*, vol. 42, no. 1
- "How He Writes those Sermons" appeared in *The Alembic*, vol. 94
- "The Last Note" appeared in *The Rockford Review*, vol. 33, no. 1
- "Matriarchs" appeared in *Tipton Poetry Journal*, issue 14
- "My Mother's Last Days" appeared in *Free XpresSion*, vol. 16, no. 10
- "The Needle" appeared in *Stand, vol. 12, no. 1*
- "Passacaglia " appeared in *Neon Literary Magazine*, vol. 38
- "People in Boxes" appeared in *Lady Churchill's Rosebud Wristlet*, vol. 34
- "Ready to Quit" appeared in *Not One of Us*, issue 42
- "Sick" appeared in *Challenger International*, vol. 12, no. 2
- "The Things that Come in the Mail" appeared in *The Deronda Review*, vol.4, no. 2
- "Three Screwdrivers Hello" appeared in *Maintenant*, vol. 6
- "The Vampire" appeared in *Extract(s)*, vol. 2
- "(won't ever) Tell on You" appeared in *Art Times*, vol. 26, no. 2

Contents

Acknowledgements — iv

Into the Cracks — 1
- At the Stop — 2
- The Rite of Exploration — 4
- The Spider in the Funeral Parlor — 5
- When They Go — 6
- In the Grip of Sensual Illusion — 7
- The White Knight — 8
- Sick — 9
- I Gave You — 10
- (won't ever) Tell on You — 11
- Bloodlines — 12
- The Mannequin's Last Stop — 13
- My Mother's Last Days — 14
- Hands Fall Like Dying Butterflies — 15
- The Daughter Who Left — 16
- Crossing Guard — 17
- On the Right Path — 18
- The Far Side of the Morning — 19
- Matriarchs — 20
- Down to the Water — 21
- Ready to Quit — 22
- The Book — 23
- Happily — 24
- Dismantled — 25
- Three Screwdrivers Hello — 26
- Listening — 27
- The Sound of Speed — 28
- Functional — 29

Now I Can Accept You	30
The Dreams of Tiny Things	31
The First Year Out	32
The Things that Come in the Mail	33
Barricade	34
Foundations Will Crumble	35
The Vampire	36
Coming Home from the Hospital	37
Bleeding the Brakes Dry	38
Your Hand in Mine	39
The Arrogant Imposter	40
Like Snakes on Hot Asphalt	41
The Last Note	42
On Finding the Man	43
The Hatchlings	44
Disintegration	45
The Needle	46
Passacaglia	47
Dacnomania	48
People in Boxes	49
Good Old Me	50
How He Writes those Sermons	51
Splintered	52
Sunshine on the Rubble	53
Laika	54
Frog Princesses	55

Into the Cracks

At the Stop

I take the dog out to the bus stop
to wait for my daughter to come home from school.
One of the other mothers has driven to the bus stop,
and she sits in her car with the windows rolled up
maybe she's listening to music,
or just enjoying the quiet.

The dog starts digging at something
and I push at her with my foot
make her stop, this isn't her yard.
She sits down and wags her tail
pushes against my leg for comfort.
I pet her large, blocky head
tell her the bus is coming soon.

I look up and see the woman in the car is watching me,
I think. She's wearing mirrored sunglasses
and I can't tell if she's watching me or just fallen asleep,
her head pressed against the window, jaw slightly open
as though something I'm doing is really interesting,
or maybe she's just slipped into a coma
or she's dead.

The school bus pulls up and I wait to see
if the woman moves
if I have to carefully walk her daughter to the car
to see what's wrong
if I have to brace her little girl for the horrible news
that her mother
has just died, right there,
sitting in the car
waiting for her to come home

and how wonderful would that be, I think,
as I see the woman straighten up and
unlock the doors of her car with a noisy "click,"
to be able to claim

to be such a devoted mother
that even though you knew something was really, really wrong,
that you really should go to the doctor instead
you still got in your car and drove to the bus stop
just to wait for your little girl to come home.

The Rite of Exploration

You make me want to drill holes in my skull
wrap wires around my brain, sink drill bits and fingertips into
my body, map the lace of fine blood vessels
with radioactive dyes, trace my skeleton through my skin
with melted solder and #2 pencils
dig a place inside me for you to curl up and sleep
never leave. I want you to have it all:

my skin to wrap in a sheet around your shoulders
or around your waist when you step out of the bath
my skull and pelvis to prop open the door
when you need to bring new furniture into the house
fingers and toes to shim under wobbly table legs and chairs
the rest of my blood to stain the floor more evenly
to match the spot on the wood where I fell.

The Spider in the Funeral Parlor

The spider does not recognize the woman as human
as it crawls across her stiff, starched collar
en route to the dark corner of the open coffin. There is nothing here
that would tell it that this is a person, no warmth
emanating from her flesh, no pulse beneath the pale, white skin,
no blood. The spider might as well be crawling over
the folded hands of a marble statue, the still chest
of a toppled goliath, a jumble of broken doll parts.

If the spider were to recognize the woman
as such, would it surmise that her blood had been removed
by something like itself, some massive creature that drained blood
from its victims, replacing bodily fluids with corrosive liquid and
leaving the outer shell of the corpse to fade in on itself
slowly, as though collapsed by a slow leak or a steady hand?
And would our little spider fear this creature that could drain
something as large as this dead woman? would it
look elsewhere than the coffin for a safe place for its web,
perhaps continue on to the far corner of the chapel instead?

When They Go

I open my arms and call my children to me, remind them
that nothing bad ever happens so long as I'm holding them.
My daughter wrinkles her nose at me and rolls her eyes, my son
just ignores me and walks away. I am no longer regarded as sanctuary
a bulwark against precocious misery and frustration: they don't need me at all.
I close my arms, wrap myself in an empty embrace

dream of being the sort of mother children flock to unquestioningly
a fish mother who opens her maw to engulf hordes of trusting fry
a scorpion mother carrying her ravenous children across the hot desert
a snake mother nested in a knot of wriggling coils of tiny tails and teeth
anything but what I am: incomplete without a tiny hand in mine
a sweaty head pressed against my chest, the constant need that only I can fulfill.

In the Grip of Sensual Illusion

The pop star's new album comes in the mail
and I am uncomfortably aware
that time has passed, the man on the cover has grown older.
There are memories tied up in his musical legacy, indelible fingerprints
on my childhood: my mother humming along at the kitchen sink
my father playing along quietly on his beat-up acoustic guitar

others from when I started calling the music my own: a tiny apartment
with a shitty stereo that I loved, the lights off, the music loud
blissful in my solitude, later: in bed with my first husband, eyes closed
pretending to be asleep, pretending there was nothing wrong
the pop star's then-new CD playing itself to the end in the background.

Even later: my son in my arms, face tiny and red, the last few words
from a well-worn song the lullaby that finally put him to sleep.
I take the new album to my office, pull out the various incarnations of
media bearing his name: two cassette tapes, four vinyl LPs, seven CDs,
lay them out in chronological order, like portraits of a family member
never seen, yet sorely missed.

The White Knight

The gears click as the horse
takes a step forward, lowers its head
into a patch of bright green Astroturf.
A pulse of static comes
from deep within its chest
something awful grinds
in an approximation of eating,
a sigh of contentment.

The man on the horse
makes grinding noises as well
as he lifts his arm
to pull on the reins.
He turns his grizzled face slowly
to stare, glass-eyed, at the horizon
a blank canvas
on which to build
something wonderful.

Sick

Days pass into weeks and you are still inside me
chiseling my heart into something
hard and cold and so terribly lost
I dream of the back of your head receding
every night.

You will grow smaller with time—soon, even the ragged
pull of your fingernails
sloughing through my flesh will feel
like mute butterfly wings
beating inside my head
and I can live with that.

I Gave You

My complaints are expelled in clouds of squid ink;
I'm determined to blind with my helpless anger. Darkness
swirls around me in a cloud, obscures the view
of the sink full of dishes, the bills stacked on the table
toys that refuse to move from where dropped

messy handprints on everything. I long
to compress myself, boneless, escape
through the drain, through the tiny cracks in the floor tile,
slither behind the stove where the mice make noise
find freedom in the dark parts of the yard
beneath the floorboards of the basement.

(won't ever) Tell on You

    insides crawl under your
    talented fingertips, pray to die before
    you get too close, find my heart

    go away, memories of him
    one place I've visited too
    many times no, I've got

    to wake up and scream again
    blind hands find the water and
    half-empty bottle of sleeping pills, dreams

    of family reunions fade
    thick drunk eyes disappear, morning
    is too far away.

Bloodlines

The maple sends its helicopter seeds across the yard
in desperation dreams of propagation. I rake most of them up
rip out the long roots of the ones that slip past me
the ones that take root and try to grow. I sometimes wonder

if my tree hates me, if it feels angry when it sees me
come out to the garden with my gardening shears
clipping its offspring close to the ground

or if it's resigned itself to the fact that it will never be surrounded
by a forest of its own family. I think of these violent acts of mine
during heavy storms when the limbs of the tree whip around my roof,

wonder if it's using the wind and the lightning as an excuse
to drop branches and clumps of leaves on my lawn,
if it's aiming for me and my children
in an act of retaliation so unexpected and sly
it can't possibly be blamed.

The Mannequin's Last Stop

her arms break off and the waves take them away,
roll them down the beach over and over until they're gone.
I wonder what the seals and dolphins will think
when they see those white, disembodied hands

reaching out to them from the depth, if they'll recognize them
as having belonged to some facsimile of a human,
some amusement to frighten each other with, build ghost stories around
or if they'll confuse them for some new type of coral.

eventually, lesser sea creatures will seek out the ceramic limbs,
scallops and limpets will bind their shells
to the insides of worn elbow joints, while anemones and sea stars
and velvet-black sea slugs will make new homes in the holes and pits
made by careless forklift tines and clumsy delivery men.

My Mother's Last Days

    I slip the bracelet into my pocket
    try the ring on my finger
    catch myself in the mirror
    see her sleeping behind me.
    My mother sleeps in the other room
    a small, sad thing huddled in a web of IV lines.

    At home, I empty my purse out, my pockets,
    put the jewelry in a drawer
    of photographs and dried corsages.
    Someday she'll be gone

    too soon.

Hands Fall Like Dying Butterflies

Let's call this love: the waves folding over your head
like the wings of a tent flap, the suffocating confines
of warm blankets in a morning you don't remember entering
the heavy arm of a stranger thrown over your chest that won't let you go.
This, let's call this last breath: home, the sinking resignation

of concrete boots pulling you across the threshold into the kitchen
the anchors that tie you to the stove, the ballast bags of screaming children
that know who you are and why you're here
even if you don't. Here, this place you belong

we'll draw a circle around it on the map
so you know where you're supposed to be, a tiny point engulfed
in winged possibilities that you will never know, those dreams
will not be allowed to hatch.
There are alarms set to different times all through this house
and your feet know when and where to take you to answer them all.

The Daughter Who Left

Reconstruct that last day: her,
standing in the doorway, suitcase in hand
straining to leave as though strapped to us,
always tearful in her memories
reluctant gratitude behind closed eyes, but so anxious to get out.

She is everywhere in this house, frozen behind picture frames
trapped in a smile that changes every time the smudged glass is dusted
sometimes, she is happy. Mostly, she is barely tolerant.

There are conversations half-remembered that take on new meaning
each time they're replayed, new depth: wisdom beyond the years
of an unhappy five-year-old, harbinger to the years
of dead silence far ahead.

Crossing Guard

the crossing guard waits
until the children enter the building
before removing his head.

his eyes close,
lips go slack
pale.

I think I could be happy
if I could remove my head
get rid of my sad, heavy brain,
savaged by electricity
silly little pills.

I can never tell
if he can see anything without his head
so I wave to him from my window,
just in case.

On the Right Path

In this room written entirely on paper
there is comfort in the nodding and agreeing of flowers; they
tell me that I am not just a crazy woman sitting alone
rambling about dark matter to an invisible audience
sketching out the history of myth in thread and canvas

tumbling inward into myself like a monk
quiet, at peace.

My daughter says she's worried about me
being alone all the time, wants to know
what I've been writing but I won't show her.
Someday, I will reveal the secrets
to the future of humanity to her, the origin of snails
the language of pills. But not now.

The Far Side of the Morning

velvet among the blue-green river rushes, you will come down with me
with the tiny frogs that dart like black velvet cats, cilia and skulls
the smooth river rocks that separate blunt, white teeth

among the bright shards of crystal flowers, the wan stalks
of purring marigolds, the bright yellow marsh streams of fog
that divide the land of white river rocks and the suction of wet mud.

I will rip the flesh from your thin, white rose petal skin
kicking and screaming, I will tell you all about this place.

Matriarchs

the battle lines have been drawn
and my aunt is winning. The other sisters
and in-laws have been feuding for the title of matriarch
in anticipation of my grandmother's
final trip to the hospital, tending to her still-breathing corpse
like well-intentioned vultures, cultivating grace
with an open hand to the crown,

back on the home front, my mother
frets that I don't take on as much visible
responsibility as my sisters-in-law do
that I've slunk into the background
way too much. My husband
wonders why we always get family news
last, blames his busy work schedule
our overwhelming kids.

I tell him
we're holding down our own fort
we have our own world, separate from my family's.
I plan ways for us to relocate to foreign countries,
send résumés to far-away companies,
long for the day when there's distance between us
and the melodrama of the front lines.

Down to the Water

If I close my eyes, I can feel the sand beneath my bare feet
the splash of imaginary fish beneath a drunk, full moon
the thin screech of seagulls in the wind.
I open my eyes and find
I am a thousand miles from any beach,
an October lawn crunching beneath my feet
thin, yellow blades of grass stiff with frost.

This is not my home. I can almost smell the sweet salt ocean air,
promises of warmer weather in the sanctuary of the car.
Winding cliff roads along rocky beaches call me, half a continent away
just past miles of pro-life billboards splashed with pictures of babies
cryptic, threatening Bible verses
that may or may not have anything to do with
the particular stretch of highway they loom over,
past miles of barbed wire separating me from herds of cows
flocks of displaced ostriches.

Ready to Quit

I wake up and it means I'm not dead. Sunlight.
Dried Flowers. Frost fingers cross the windowpane
and I am alive, fuck you, fuck you one more
day. I say fuck you, good morning, and I'm alive.

Feet and I glide the floor the kitchen, effortlessly, I'm flying.
Oooo, I'm a ghost. No, I'm awake. Cereal. Coffee
pulsing in my veins, hangover, at least he didn't spend the night.
Goodbye common sense. Hello mister penis.
If only the memories
would leave as easily as the words do.

Feel free to look through my underwear drawer. Hello strange man,
strange men in my roomy room room. Feel free to guess
how much change is in the jar on my dresser.
Chew toys in my bathroom and no dog
in the apartment? I could be a wacko. Better watch out!
Where does the poetry fit in? Will I write about this?
Will I write about this?

I'm awake and it means I'm not dead. Aspirin. Orange juice.
Sunlight. Crow's feet grow as I watch in the mirror
my eyes my eyes I am alive, fuck you, fuck you, fuck you,
I say fuck you, good morning, I am alive.

The Book

Cut off by the book's tattered seam, the wind blows
the curtains in, calling his billowing skin down
back to where it belongs.

It's years later, I'm still at the palazzo
lying in ruins just behind the ghost of the man
skinned for this fish story.

Happily

    typewriter lies dead in the corner
    on the floor, keys scattered like a mouthful
    of angry teeth inlaid with
    carefully-set letters of ebony
    screaming
    "hit me again you
    qwerty motherfucker"

Dismantled

He said she was the one and checked under her dress;
she found him hard and improper, evil
all over his parts. He wrapped himself around her as though
she had already passed on, whispering about other girls he had killed
this very way.

There were years and years woven into his hair, she could see
her future unraveling in those long strands of light.
She would never again walk alone down by the water
in the evening, whistling at birds and befriending trees
she would grow pale and emaciated under his trembling fingers
fade until only her bones were left.

Three Screwdrivers Hello

I pushed carts for six years before
reaching my destination. The gorilla suit
was tight and itchy and
much too warm to wear in the summer.
I don't know how many times I had to stop,
strip down, and spread out on the sand
just to remember the shape of my body.

I'll bet if you put all my dreams in one pocket
you'd have room enough for bus fare in change.
I get like a razor when you say you
"understand," mock the lonely inside me
as I bind scraped skin together. There are
too many other lost people out there
for me to be fooled by your sympathy.

Listening

    In the shadows of derelict trains, four bloody fingertips
    tumble into a pile, disordered as books
    balanced on the head of a sad librarian. The donor,
    arms around God, will remind you of these fingertips
    on the day you meet her
    on your first sunrise as a fresh body in the morgue
    on that day you believe you will be able to go anywhere

    because of the few memorable good deeds
    you've performed, your repeated acts
    of contrition. When you get tired of carrying her fingers in your pocket
    pretending that you were the one who severed them from her hand
    in some bizarre rite of manhood, you will have to find a new place
    to hide them, perhaps in the folds of a stranger's sofa,
    a dentist's lobby, stuffed into the cavity
    of a patient during open heart surgery,
    in the bottom of the kitchen trash.

The Sound of Speed

Even through the splintering of wood and the thunder of passing trains
I can hear you in the dark, the rush, the roar of your heart
a desperate bird struggling to fly free, up and past
the flickering bare bulb swinging over the bed.

I spread my hands wide over your chest to soothe
the frightened bird, imagine arteries and muscles
wrapping you in great blues wires and metal bridge cables
straining to keep everything in place

the scraping of muscle and skin, the sparks
the screech of angry brakes
the silence.

Functional

when I first began to feel my mind slip
I told my mother, she said
there were ways to hide my problem
make lists, schedules
turn myself into a functional robot
and it would pass.

when it got worse, I told my husband
he said, "you can't do this
remember you're a mother
we're all depending on you."
he said if I went nuts
he would leave

and so I spent my children's youth
stumbling from one drugged haze to another
test-running medications that made
my fingers twitch, my skin itch
checking off my daily duties
on lists made the night before.
functional.

when I first began to feel my mind slip
I longed to be locked away
in some meadow-surrounded provincial madhouse
like the ones I had seen on TV.
it was only when I was older
trapped in domestic bliss
that I realized real people
don't get that kind of break.

Now I Can Accept You

In those holding-hands photographs of us on my parents' wall
time has begun to leach the color from you, and only you, as though
you had already pulled your roots out of me, even then.
I feel myself growing smaller just speaking your name out loud
in the complete quiet that follows the memories of a childhood love.

I don't know how to find the wounds I'm dying from
buried somewhere in these memories of half-spoken promises.
You are everything good and warm to me,
a summer full of memories, an irresistible force
hiding under my heart

The Dreams of Tiny Things

The birds outside my window speak
of world domination, the tiny gray sparrows have staked out
my kitchen for their future headquarters. They fly
right up to my window so they can look
inside my house, stare into my kitchen
chirp angrily to one another about how wasteful I am
sweeping stray breadcrumbs into the trash,
mutter about how things will be different once
I am out of the house.

The squirrels in the yard are in it with the birds,
but they have larger demands, a larger scope of conquest.
Today, their view of domination concerns taking over
only a couple of houses, or maybe even a couple of square blocks
of old, crumbling, Depression-era residences. They scamper up
to my office window, put tiny brown paws against the glass,
take stock of my desk drawers stuffed with loose paper
perfectly suited for building nests, raising pink, hairless babies,
hiding out from the long winter ahead.

The First Year Out

>Numbers of geese flew overhead and you laughed at my excitement, our mutual relief
>at the sight of the old farm still standing, the broken windmill, the outlying buildings.
>They held a future we'd dreamed aloud—a vegetable garden,
>flocks of chickens and turkeys thick as clouds and eager for morning.
>Your fingertips massaged the ache that had settled into my shoulders
>so many years ago I'd lost count.

>The ache set into new places, almost forgotten, for a while longer,
>for a full season of wonder
>as we made final promises against a sun that kept disappearing
>as if into a great crack in a wall of re-occurring rainbows. You told me about the geese
>that would land in the new pond and stay, the cows that were coming soon.
>You spoke as if we had a real destination, a plan.

>I am still holding onto that first day, descending over barren hills
>borders between states disappearing into thin spiderwebs crisscrossing a map—
>sacred ash in a smoldering iron pot. I remember when you laid out
>your theory of the sun-scorched, explained how we
>were just like those clouds of birds that came to rest on the flat, golden plains around us
>their feathers taunting us for our slow, tired bondage to earth.
>It all made so much sense back then.

The Things that Come in the Mail

the flowers come in the mail, with the cards, with the lovely notes
expressing sympathy for our loss. I don't want to answer the door anymore
want to let the tiny wreaths pile up, wither away.

I smile, thank the delivery man for my mail,
I smile at my husband, I smile at everyone.
I call relatives to let them know I'm fine, I don't need
anything. I thank them for their kindness and for the flowers.
my husband compliments me on my strength, I reply with
another smile. my face hurts from smiling so much. at night

I find myself talking to the missing baby, holding
my hands over my stomach, protecting nothing. I shuffle through
these days, find comfort in repetitive tasks. I vacuum constantly.
I crochet mittens for everyone. I turn inside myself

hold back everything but this smile, the one I show my family
my husband—it's all I've got left.

Barricade

I pretend my house is an island,
Louisiana before the white men came
surrounded by the emptiness of the ocean and virginal
in the ways of casual conversation.
The wind blows in the sound of trains rumbling by
sounds like voices coming through a baby monitor,
strange hands
poised to smash through glass.

I am San Juan before the Spanish landed,
far from the boy next door
and the thud of the dishwasher upstairs.
I can almost see all the way to Catalina Island
through the flocks of white-winged
the glare of streetlights and storm clouds
heavy with portent. The ripple of galleon sails

distorts the horizon, damns me to admit
white men once continued long enough down the Mississippi
to find my house, did not turn around
at the entrance of the Gulf of Mexico, were not dissuaded
by the piles of beer cans in my trash,
the oil derricks tilted off-center in the bay
the lawn paved over to make a cracked basketball court.

Foundations Will Crumble

We pass each other once, twice a year
my old friends, my getting-older friend—
chance encounters at the grocery store, brief escapes
to the bar. We barely recognize each other,
so much time has passed. We fumble with words
to express appreciation for new hairstyles
a recent manicure, minor accomplishments
tiptoeing around the subject
of the aches and pains of our decay.

Buildings and civilizations rise from the dust
flourish and die just outside my house
as I fold laundry, cook dinner
straighten the same damned pillows
again and again, send out emails, make phone calls
to the outside world, to remind the few people
who still remember me

that I'm still here.

The Vampire

The vampire
comes in through my window and sees
I have written more poems about him.
He leans against the wall, in the shadows,
brow furrowed
as he thumbs through the pages, leaves

bloody fingerprints

on the crumpled edges. I watch him
from my bed, eyes half-closed
watch him as he shakes his head,
snorts derisively,

scribbles something nasty

in the corner of one sheet, crosses out
all the words I've used improperly
with a bright red pen.

Coming Home from the Hospital

She bumps against me in the seat and I wonder
what would happen if I took her, this girl
too young to be riding on the bus by herself
too young to be so close to so many strangers.
I smile and scoot over farther to make room for her to sit

imagine she's my daughter, that I have a daughter
slight, blond-haired, green eyes like mine
wonder if the other passengers already think she's here with me.
I press myself up against the latched window
wonder what our life would be like together
I could pop the emergency release
grab her and run.

Bleeding the Brakes Dry

    I can almost feel the warm water pooling
    around my sore ankles, the burnt skin on the tops of my feet;
    far away is a safe place where tiny crustaceans wriggle beneath
    my heel in time with the ebb of the tide. If I try hard enough

    the rumble of waves crashing on a white sand beach are loud enough
    that I can't hear the angry muttering in the garage, the sound
    of my car being worked on by a husband who promised
    to take me away from here, take me back to the ocean
    so long ago it might as well be a lie.

Your Hand in Mine

Leaves appear on trees as conversations
slowly unfold, green, between us
as timorous as field mouse paws
resting delicately on plastic garbage bags
filled with possibility.

I long to face this spring dead-on, reconstruct
these last death throes of love
as anything but.

The Arrogant Imposter

he ate, pushing his fork into the pile of spaghetti
in front of him with a fervor that seemed
too angry for dinner. he was nervous, my father
was out of town and he
was not supposed to be there.

my mother watched him eat with the look of
a contented lion in her eyes, this was her
plan come true, her lover at the table with us
her children, we could pretend to be a family

while my dad was gone. He tried to engage me
in talk about school, about what I wanted to be
when I grew up, what sorts of things I liked
smiling too big as my mother's knee touched his
under the table. There were things I wanted to say
things I should have said

but my mind went blank, my tongue numb when I
saw him take my mother's hand.

Like Snakes on Hot Asphalt

My father's horizon was always
Kansas, he never grew past being
a tiny spot surrounded by miles
of cattle-flattened silage
and stunted sagebrush.

I don't know the names of any
of my inborn horizons, can only guess
at who lives in the row of small, dark houses
across the street. I am also an unnecessary pinpoint
surrounded by flat, black asphalt
waves of heat reflected off the crumbling tar.

I remember the road trips to ocean surf
the reverent look on my father's face
as he realized, again and again
that the world was so much more
than hot tar and dead cornfields.

"All you gotta do is get in your car and drive," he'd marvel
a sudden world explorer, a world conqueror
wearing a grin big enough to smash giants.

The Last Note

If Houdini could not make it back
from the afterlife
to let his waiting wife know he had crossed over
that there was a heaven
or that he was in hell
or nothing at all
then you should not expect to hear from me
after I'm gone. Leave no

spirit bells by the window for me to ring
do not look for my face in the shadowed corners
reflected in mirrors, bring no
spirit-channelers to ghost-write one last
love letter to you from beyond the grave

don't look for me
for I won't be there.

On Finding the Man

the dog finds the man first, sniffs
at the pool of blood by his hand. in its mythology
this man is always upright, noisy,
exuding clouds of purple tobacco smoke
never still and quiet. the death of this man
does not fit into the dog's cosmology
is a crushing blow to its faith.

later, birds find the man, tiny sparrows
drawn to the clouds of nits and flies
already building great fortresses in his blood-caked hair
claiming him for various
insect kingdoms. crows settle, chase sparrows away
flick aside the flies, the arraying, wiggling maggots
dig past the layer of dried flesh and blood
find rapture in fresh meat.

The Hatchlings

    it unfurls from its egg, fish messiah
    spreads translucent fins wide and sails into the river.
    behind it, siblings follow suit, tentatively abloom in the water
    follow the first-born's gospel of escape.

    years from now, when all but a handful have survived
    this one moment will be sharp in their subconscious:
    a song of rebirth in the raspy breath of the wind
    the pull of the current against their new flesh.

Disintegration

    to prevent my arm from falling
    a staff holds my hand up
    a truss binds my shoulder. the cloak
    covers my distress like wallpaper
    over a cracked foundation, a thin, necessary veneer
    to show I am closer to alive than dead.

    to prevent my mouth from sagging, I have wrapped wire
    around the top and bottom hedge
    of broken teeth, practice smiling
    with closed lips and bloody gums.

The Needle

if you could play your fingerprints
with a phonograph needle
what do you think your song would be?
is there an SOS of pops and snaps
in the ridges of your thumbs
or is there an overture waiting to be heard
buried in the whorls of your index finger?

if you could play your skin like a slab
of mint vinyl, would your flaws resound joyous
in bagpipes and flutes, would your wrinkles sound like the ocean
would your calluses rock hard?

or would it all be a mess

some unlistenable cacophony
a recording of your failures
silent angers
old age?

Passacaglia

I trudge from the bedroom to the kitchen every morning, hands ready
to make food, fix clothing, brush hair. There is no questioning
my role in this dance, which steps I must take—the required pirouettes
are worn into the carpet as visibly as if someone had outlined my feet in chalk.

The school bus leaves and I turn once, twice,
fetch the newspaper from the stoop, go inside, make coffee.
The birds outside the kitchen window watch me move
imitate my shuffle on the lip of the bird feeder, mock me
with their fluttering wings, their tiny, sure feet,
their perfectly coiffed feathers.

I long to find the recordings that dictate my moves
the slow-paced funereal marches that decide my day.
I don't know what I'd do with them
except make them stop.

Dacnomania

when we pray to dark gods to bring wonderful things, we must be prepared
to accept the consequences. when we make deals with devils
pray to the things that crawl beneath our feet
even if just for tiny hands, a warm bundle wrapped in flannel
tiny eyelashes and soft, pink cheeks
we must accept that whatever comes from such a deal

may be flawed. those tiny hands might not rest as well
at night as they should, might flounder about in sleep
grasping for the phantom pickaxes and knives
that will fit so well into them when they're grown, those tiny, perfect feet
kicking comically in the dark might be kicking in a door someday,
breaking through wood
to get at some screaming huddle hiding just beyond.

remember all of this, that this was all your idea
this late night trek to the cemetery to bargain, this
searching through old books for that one, specific spell
the things you asked for when you slid your fistful of dollars
across the old witch's table—when the time comes, remember
this is your fault.

People in Boxes

    cracked leather stretched over
    matchstick bones, the outlines of deer and
    water deities turned light blue with time
    scrawled along the arms and legs of a forgotten
    priest or poet or king with the point
    of a blade or the tip of a pin
    dipped in ink and stuck in, again and again
    the long-legged blond woman wearing antlers on her head
    the short, bearded man frozen into the mountain
    the little girl, curled up in sleep beneath a poncho
    decorated with pictures of alpaca, skin punctured
    by eagle claws
    who are these people scattered random through the steppes?

    a blackened hand with two fingernails left
    hard and perfect, wisps of reddish-brown hair spread
    in a cloud around emaciated, desert-tanned shoulders
    palm out, frozen in salute, greeting
    an audience centuries late, the bones of former servants
    favorite pets, a pair of horses still strapped
    to an ornate chariot
    spread out in an arc of waste, circling
    a stone sarcophagus, an ice-filled wooden coffin
    a painted oblong packaged and muffled in layers of resin and cloth
    a cave so high in the mountains that there is no
    returning from the climb—these are the people
    that will outlast history
    not poets.

Good Old Me

    the memories are scrawled in books, scattered
    all around my house, as if left by some drunk—

    ramblings, all of them!
    (Here's one more faded scrap.) The first five minutes
    of a story about my favorite cat (she died
    painfully of lung cancer when I was four) here's
    something about husband #1 (closet

    homosexual, came out soon after our son
    was born) here's the first page of a
    hospital diary (with baby struggling for life because
    he didn't know he would just end up coming
    home with me) who

    is this person leaving these things
    lying around for just anybody to read?

How He Writes those Sermons

he said he could take it or leave it, or maybe it was
some other trite cliché, laughing at me
as though i'd given him dogshit for his birthday
as though i was dogshit. i waited until church was over
before sneaking out past the rest of my family
i wanted to hide somewhere. i wanted to cry.

there were memories born in the garage out back
that i wished dead, i could give or take them, too
if i could, except i couldn't take back those fingers
his hot breath on my neck, i could still smell his wreck
on my skin. i wiped myself down after he left

thought of his birthday, how now we were together
thought of his birthday and what i could give him
something else, something i hadn't given him already
i could take or leave that memory, too. "come,"
my mom said right away, right when she came out
saw me red-faced and angry standing alone
her usual after-church socializing forgotten.
she was quiet all the way home.

Splintered

    piece of scrap. metal flakes, a thin silver curl
    an unconscious sculpture, an arm
    moves overhead, a face, a flower, the magnet
    still stained with blood, a steering column

    sharp as a pin, a razor blade. wheels crush overhead
    bending metal pinion around metal pinion
    pulls the loose scrap up, sharp edged
    metal scrapes, drags against other metal
    one second of realism. wheels
    a door

Sunshine on the Rubble

We approach each other's present-day
as civilizations in decline, look beyond
the conquered walls and shattered windows
scars carved in flesh by unmentionable acts
remnants of wars that must be acknowledged
but written and spoken only as
fixed, immutable points in the past.

instead, we revel in the struts left standing
despite the damage, point out the fine detailing
in frescoed hallways and ornamental lintels
find beauty in even the most accidental of places:

a line of tiny flowers blooming in a sidewalk crack
a spray of green lichen obscuring decades of decay
a statue of a girl I used to be, still standing guard
over the last of the locked doors
I will open only for you.

Laika

The little girl with the puppy on tv
looks so sad as she hands her dog over
to the men who will put it in a box
send it into space
make it the first dog in space. Behind her
her parents look so proud, they are so proud

to be the owners of this dog who will be
the first dog in space. I wonder

what stories they told their daughter
when they talked her into letting the stray she'd rescued
be a part of the space program, if they
filled her head with images of Laika
navigating his way around his very own
dog-sized spaceship, punching brightly-lit buttons
issuing reports back to Earth
about what it was like
to be in space, about all the wonderful things

he could see way up there
through the porthole window

and I wonder how awful she must have felt
years later, if and when she realized
how terrified her puppy must have felt
floating weightless, confused, in that tiny box
sent to die so far from home, far from her
and if he thought he was there
because he'd done something wrong

like peeing on the rug
or eating her homework.

Frog Princesses

I watch my daughter playing in the yard
singing to earthworms and dancing with toads
and I know she sees all the magical things
I'm missing. I join in on her games
make fairy houses out of mud and broken seashells

share stories of how wonderful it would be
if we were frogs or fairies ourselves
and I can tell she believes
we could be those things if we really wanted to be
and that being just what we are is some sort of choice
I can tell she believe this
and I wish I could, too.

www.ingramcontent.com/pod-product-compliance
Lightning Source LLC
Chambersburg PA
CBHW052207110526
44591CB00012B/2118